Making the Impossible Possible

A Step By Step Guide For Achieving Your Most Challenging Goals

Joe Stumpf

The Yellow Umbrella

Once upon a time, a young man set out on a journey to discover his life's mission.

He wandered the Earth for several decades, seeking ways to make his mark in the world. Whenever he completed a mission, he immediately felt compelled to seek yet another.

Then one day he came upon a wise teacher who was sitting on a hillside under a **Yellow Umbrella.**

The seeker asked the teacher, "I am seeking my true life's mission. Can you help me find it?"

The wise teacher smiled. "You are a seeker, are you not?"

He replied, "My life has been about seeking ways to impact others in a positive way, usually with things that most people consider to be impossible."

With a smile on his face, the wise teacher replied, "You are a seeker and you are doing what is natural for a seeker. Perhaps you have not accepted the truth that your life mission is to seek because to find would mean you would no longer exist. Once you accept this truth, you will fully embrace the life of a seeker and let go of the notion that you are here to find."

The wise teacher reached up and handed the **Yellow Umbrella** to the man and said, "This is yours now – pass it on to the next seeker who asks how they can find their life's mission."

This guide is for the seeker in you. May you embrace this beautiful aspect of yourself and once you do, please pass it on.

Dedicated To My Daughters-

I was asked by a smart man, "What would you die for?" The answer was simple: my daughters. I wanted to add my freedom, my honor, my faith, and my country, but I don't really know if that is true. Every day, Traci and Olivia teach me a little bit more about how to love, laugh, and live.

Traci said to me recently, "Dad, I want to be your social media director. Just because you can deadlift a Ramada Inn doesn't mean you know how to get Instagram followers."

Then she posted a Boomerang video and within one hour, 600 people liked it (**instagram.com/joestumpf**).

She said, "Dad, we all have our strengths." Traci is a successful comic host. Check her out at **TraciStumpf.com**

Olivia is my wise Buddha baby.

Whenever I have a complex personal choice to make, she is the first person I turn to for insight. Like her mother, Cathy, she has a way of cutting through to the truth with just a few words.

For example, I told her about my challenge, living in a more rural area where I didn't have many casual connections.

She calmly smiled, walked over to me, gave me a hug, and whispered in my ear, "Dad, you've mastered the casual relationship. Maybe it's time to learn how to have a deep relationship with yourself." Truth!

She's a yoga teacher and amazing Spin teacher. She loves helping people discover their fitness and health—just like her daddy.

When you're in the Los Angeles area, drop in and see her at YAS in Los Feliz. She'll help you sweat it out (**facebook.com/OliviaStumpf**).

Here's What's Inside...

Making The Impossible Possible

I got my basic training in "Making the Impossible Possible" at the age of 10. It was a three-year training program every Sunday at 7:00 pm.

My father and four siblings would gather in the TV room, each of us with a bowl of Jiffy Pop®; Dad's bowl was always super-sized. Clutching our bowls, we all sank into the old orange leather couch. For the next hour, our eyes were glued to the Zenith TV, watching his favorite show, *Mission: Impossible.*

The character of Jim Phelps, played by Peter Graves, was the head of the IMF, a super-secret government agency. The show would start with Phelps in a phone booth or some back alley with a file and a tape recorder. He'd look over the picture as the voice on the tape would describe the mission.

At the end of the message, the voice would say, "Jim, as always, if you choose to accept this mission, and if you or any of your team are caught or killed, the secretary will disavow any knowledge of your existence. Good luck, Jim! As always, this tape will self-destruct in five seconds." Then the fuse was lit and the famous Mission Impossible theme song would play. In the next scene, Jim would be picking his team, depending on which tasks needed to be done, and always relying on high-tech equipment and elaborate deceptions.

There was one turning-point scene in every episode when they took off the mask and revealed one of the team members disguised as somebody else. Usually, at the end of each episode, you got to enjoy the bad guys' realization that he had been out-done by the skillful planning of the IMF team.

By 8:00 pm, everyone's popcorn is long gone; what seemed impossible only an hour earlier, had become possible.

In the hour it takes you to read this book, my goal is for you to create your "Mission: Impossible". I will help you to imagine applying my Secret Formula that I've created for you to make it possible. (*A secret is something everyone knows, but few apply.*)

And, as always, if you choose not to read the entire book and implement the steps to make your impossible possible, I will dissolve any knowledge of your being.

Relax. I'm just kidding.

But seriously, in the hour it takes to read this book, I'll share my direct experience of making the impossible possible.

My hope is that, once you conceive the impossible, you will accept the mission.

Chapter 1: My Impossible Mission

In early September 2012, I was having breakfast with Justin Arnst at the Encinitas Cafe on a Sunday morning. I had met Justin during my KOKORO experience a year earlier.

At the time, Justin owned a CrossFit gym in Sacramento, California. CrossFit is the ultimate test of fitness. It measures your strength, endurance, power, and speed across all domains. You are tested for running, biking, swimming, gymnastics, weightlifting, powerlifting and odd objects, moving far and fast, and every body movement you can imagine.

During breakfast, Justin said, "You know there's this thing called the CrossFit Games Open, where they have this global contest. This is the first year they're having a master's division for guys who are 55 to 59, and you ought to do it."

I said, "I ought to do what?" He said, "You could qualify for the Games. I know you can!"

The right words, from the right person, at the right time.

Mission conceived.

He told me, "Today is the last day to register and record your score for the first of five workouts. You can do this and you should do this. It's only $10."

I said, "Let's do it now." He took out his cell phone, opened the app, and he registered me for the 2012 CrossFit Open Games.

Mission accepted.

Then he said, "Let's go to the gym right now and do **Workout #1.**" (i.e. the maximum number of burpees in seven minutes.)

That's all the information I had, so I did 100 burpees in seven minutes.

Now I had no idea how good or bad of a score that was until the next day when I looked at the global rankings. My 100 burpees in seven minutes had me ranked #23 in the world.

I thought if I did the work, I could be one of the top 20 to qualify.

Starting to form a belief.

Belief comes easier when you conceive an idea and you get an early positive validation.

A word of caution.

A new idea is like the seed just planted. It needs good soil, sunshine, water, and encouragement. Justin was my encouragement.

If I would have shared it with someone who didn't think it was a good idea and they had said, "That will be really hard and your chance of making it is very slim," they would have sown doubt.

Have you ever conceived an exciting idea and shared it with a raven? A raven is a person who devours the seed before it has time to take root. Thankfully, Justin was not a raven. This is what happened over the next five weeks.

Workout #2

- 45-pound Snatch, 30 reps.
- 75-pound Snatch, 30 reps.
- 100-pound Snatch, 30 reps.
- 120-pound Snatch, as many reps as possible in 10 minutes.

I ranked 13th after workout #2.

Workout #3
Complete as many rounds and reps of the following as possible in 18 minutes:

- 15 Box jumps or step-ups, 20" box.
- 95-pound Push press, 12 reps.
- 9 Toes-to-bar.

I moved into 12th place after workout #3.

Workout #4

Complete as many reps as possible in seven minutes following the rep scheme below:

- 90-pound Thruster, 3 reps.
- 3 Chest to bar Pull-ups.
- 90-pound Thruster, 6 reps.
- 6 Chest to bar Pull-ups.
- 90-pound Thruster, 9 reps.
- 9 Chest to bar Pull-ups.
- 90-pound Thruster, 12 reps.
- 12 Chest to bar Pull-ups.
- 90-pound Thruster, 15 reps.
- 15 Chest to bar Pull-ups.
- 90-pound Thruster, 18 reps.
- 18 Chest to bar Pull-ups.
- 90-pound Thruster, 21 reps.
- 21 Chest to bar Pull-ups.

I dropped to 20th place.

Workout #5

Complete as many rounds and reps as possible in 12 minutes of the following:

- 150 Wall balls (20 lbs to 9' target).
- 90 Double-unders.
- 30 Muscle-ups.

Back then, I could not do a muscle-up, and I strongly believed that I could not do a muscle-up. Of course, what the thinker thinks, the prover proves; I fell to 21st place after workout #5— just 1 point away from going to the Games.

But that experience caused me to believe that it was possible for me to make it to the Games. I just needed to strengthen the belief and be willing to do whatever it took to learn muscle-ups.

What I didn't know was that it would take me five more years before I could put all the pieces together over the five workouts, and achieve it.

I love this thought: We overestimate what we can do in one year and greatly underestimate what we can do in five years. We overestimate what we can get done because to change a belief requires time and space.

To form a new belief requires doing the inner work, plus adding a team of people who believe in you. This team must believe in you as much or more than you believe in yourself.

Of course, we must have the willingness to do the work, but the belief comes first.

The Five-Year Journey

In 2013, I came in 46th place.

In 2014, I came in 187th place.

In 2015, I came in 63rd place.

Then in 2016, I came in 102nd place, but I was the second fittest 59-year-old in the world.

In 2017, I aged up to a new group: 60+. And I believed that this was my year.

Those five years were about building belief. Today, I realize that I did not fail in 2103 through 2016. I was simply working on developing the belief. How long does it take to develop belief?

Again, we overestimate what we can change in a year and massively underestimate what we can get done in five years.

In 2010, if you had told me that I would be one of the "20 Fittest Men on Earth" at the age of 60, I would have said, "Impossible!"

Yet, in April of 2017, I qualified as one of only 20 men in the world over the age of 60 to go to the CrossFit Games.

So how in the world did Joe Stumpf become one of 20 men on Earth over the age of 60 to make it to the CrossFit Games?

The facts:

In 2017, 400,000 people around the world entered the contest. Only 320 would make it to the end.

There are 40 men and 40 women in the 18 to 34 age group. There are 20 men and 20 women in each of the other age groups (35–39, 40–44, 45–49, 50–54, 55–59 and 60+). That's a total of 320 people: 160 men and 160 women.

Out of the 400,000, the 60+ group made up the smallest number of entries: 2,200 men. Only 20 men made it. Out of the 20 men who made it in the 60+ group, 12 of them had made it to the Games in previous years. So only eight out of the 2,188 men who entered had a chance to win.

So what does that say?

All of them had, at one time, probably thought it was impossible to get to the CrossFit Games. Now 12 of the 20 are going for their second, third, maybe fourth time and they're no longer thinking "Impossible." They probably had a different thought: "Not going is improbable."

This is what really made the biggest impression: I became one of only eight men to qualify for the 2017 Games for the first time!

If you had told me when I conceived the idea of qualifying for the CrossFit Games that only eight people can go for their first time, I would have said, "Impossible!" (A word of caution: when you conceive your impossible dream, it may be best that you don't know the odds of success.)

Be careful of researching the possibilities of achieving your dream; it's only information that you add to your bank of beliefs. A belief is simply a thought you have over and over again. And what the thinker thinks, the prover proves.

When we think about the difficulty level of something, our unconscious mind goes to work to prove us right.

When you are committed to making the impossible possible, ignorance is actually bliss.

Again, I don't tell you any of this to impress you. I tell you this to impress upon you the truth of this statement from Napoleon Hill's book, *Think and Grow Rich*.

Whatever the mind of man can conceive and believe, it can achieve.

What do you have the capacity to conceive?

In your life or business, what can you birth today?

What can you conceive?

What seed could you plant today that may not show up in the form of achievement until you really believe it?

You may have some amazing thoughts and conceptions, but not yet have enough belief to support their achievement.

Earl Nightingale wrote a program called the "Strangest Secret." He wrote these words:

"You become what you think about most of the time."

I heard that for the first time when I was 17 years old and I thought, "I'm going to become a girl."

What could you conceive today?

There is a moment in everyone's life when the seed is planted and you conceive an idea.

Then there is a moment in time when it gets achieved.

That achievement could happen in a year, in five or ten years, or in 20 years. It all depends upon the strength of your belief and willingness to do whatever it takes to see it through. What seemingly impossible goal have you conceived that now requires you to believe it, so that you will trigger the willingness to achieve it?

This is a truly delicious conversation.

This conversation will be about my journey that led me from conceiving the thought of being one of the 20 fittest men on Earth to achieving it—and how it was built around a belief.

I want to share with you how I built huge, strong, powerful believer muscles based on two thoughts.

Whatever the mind of man can conceive and believe, it can achieve.

We become what we think about most of the time.

Chapter 2: So, What Do You Believe?

Definition: A belief is a thought we have over and over again, which becomes true to us.

In other words, we keep repeating the thought and it becomes true.

The world is flat, the world is flat, the world is flat, the world is flat, the world is flat. The world must be flat. It must be flat, let's find out that it's flat. It is flat, it must be flat. Look, there are no maps that say it's anything but flat. It's flat, it's flat, it's flat, it's flat.

Then one guy says, "Wait a minute. I think I'm going to do something different." Christopher Columbus conceives a thought.

"I will be the man who becomes the great explorer. I will be the great explorer. I will be known as the great explorer. I will do things beyond any other sailor. I will become the great explorer."

And he assigns an identity to himself—he will be the great explorer. So what do great explorers do?

They defy belief. They go beyond what everyone else is doing, and it proves that something everyone else was thinking is not true. Suddenly, it's possible.

Everything starts out as impossible; it shifts to being possible when somebody believes it.

George Bernard Shaw said, "The reasonable man adapts himself to the world; the unreasonable man persists in trying to adapt the world to himself. Therefore, all progress depends on the unreasonable man."

Horseless Carriage: The unreasonable man, Henry Ford.

Henry Ford hated horses. Rumor has it he had been kicked a few too many times by cantankerous horses and he just didn't trust them as transportation. So, he was constantly looking for ways to get around riding a horse into town. He lived on a farm and hated it.

One day, he came across a buggy with a huge steam engine propelling it down the country road near his parents' farm, which was different than the usual horse-drawn buggy. Henry Ford, who already had a reputation for tinkering with contraptions, flagged down the rider and asked him everything he could about the machine-powered buggy.

Not too long after that, Henry Ford was seen around Detroit with his newfangled contraption—the quadricycle—and crowds followed him everywhere.

The Four-Minute Mile: The unreasonable man, Roger Bannister

Bannister wanted to win a gold medal in the 1952 Helsinki Olympics. When he finished fourth in the 1500-meter race, he was understandably upset.

After walking away from the Olympic Games without a medal in hand, he set a bigger goal for himself: to be the first man on the planet to run a four-minute mile.

At the time, it was an unheard-of goal and considered impossible.

But after training for months to improve his speed in each quarter mile, on May 6th, 1954, Bannister broke the four-minute mile by running a mile in 3 minutes and 59.4 seconds.

The iPOD: The unreasonable man, Steve Jobs

The iPod shook the world when it arrived. Suddenly, you could carry around more music than you could listen to in a week, and have the device with you everywhere.

Light Without Fire: The unreasonable man, Thomas Edison

It's no secret that Thomas Edison, the famed inventor, failed "10,000 times" before he perfected the idea of the lightbulb.

Before the lightbulb, people were reliant on lamps and candles; oil and wax were considered necessary in order to function at night. Fires were a way of life.

Man on the moon: The unreasonable man, John F. Kennedy

It's likely that we all know the story of Neil Armstrong's famous words, "One small step for man, one giant leap for mankind."

Mentioned less often is John F. Kennedy's address to Congress in 1961. He said, "I believe that this nation should commit itself to achieving the goal, before this decade is out, of landing a man on the moon and returning him safely to the earth."

In the time of Plato, Jesus, or even Leonardo da Vinci, reaching the heavens was nothing more than a dream left for the undiscovered country that is the afterlife.

Today we have not only reached the heavens, we have touched the moon.

How do you create a belief to make the impossible possible?

Start repeating it over and over again, and assign an identity to yourself as the person who has that belief.

Affirmations

Let's talk about a concept you have heard before, and shine a **new light on it**. I'm talking about affirmations.

An affirmation is a suggestion you make to yourself, a **carefully crafted** statement of a desirable intention you want to deliberately create. By consciously meditating and dwelling on it, through constantly repeating the statement and visualizing it as true, you automatically implant the affirmation so it becomes part of who you want to be.

This is how you create what you want.

The absolutely wonderful news is the scientific process of self-affirmation, in terms of positively affecting your brain. It's free to do at any time without any wacky negative side effects.

When **practiced deliberately** and repeatedly, affirmations regularly reinforce the chemical pathway used by your brain to strengthen the neurons connecting to your statement.

How Affirmations Work

Imagine that your brain is like a big, dry piece of land. When the rain comes down, the water has no place to go until it cuts a path through the land.

In front of my home, I have a large hill that is sloped towards the house. One winter, we got deluged with rain—72 inches in two months. Without a drainage system, the water just ran all over the place.

So with my shovel, I carved out a path so the water drains down into the gutter and then eventually into the ocean. The water will **cut**

deeper and deeper into the earth and down this path. The deeper the indentation made by the water, the more the water can run through it.

Your brain works the same way. When you put a thought into your brain, it's like creating small rivers out of rain. Having the same thought over and over again, attached to the same level of emotion, is like pouring more water into the same groove. The "indentation" eventually makes the thought a **natural way** of thinking by firing your neurons in a very specific pattern that fuses your synapses together.

What Makes Language Patterns Hypnotic?

You'll quickly see how **hypnotic language patterns** can be. I'll use some of these hypnotic language patterns with you right now to rewrite or create your affirmations.

This is one of the patterns I use: *I love the thought*. You will hear me say that frequently. **I love the thought**. It's called a truism because the body and mind, at a cellular level, know all truth.

Doctor David Hawkins says, "There's nothing that's false; there are only things that are more true." In his original book called *Power vs. Force*, he introduced one of the most important concepts I've integrated into my life. It's the **concept of kinesiology** and understanding how to speak the truth.

If I affirm something untrue, my body knows it. If I say, "I am a CrossFit Games Athlete," but really I am not, the body knows I'm not telling the truth and gets weak from that thought.

This is called **cognitive dissonance**.

The mind does not have the capacity to hold two opposing thoughts simultaneously. It will automatically gravitate towards the thought that is most true, and the most true thought is that I am not (yet) a CrossFit Games Athlete.

Using kinesiology, there are many ways to test whether your body is weak or strong in relation to a thought, to know whether or not it's true.

If you simply put the words "I love the thought" in front of whatever you desire, you turn the future into the truth today.

So, when I say, "I love the *thought* that I am a CrossFit Games Athlete," I am pouring water into that groove repeatedly, so the neural networks in my brain get wired together.

When I am training and I repeat over and over again, "**I love the thought that** I am a CrossFit Games Athlete," I am aligning myself to make the thought of being a CrossFit Games Athlete into my current reality.

Just by using the phrase *"I love the thought"* in front of all my affirmations, I have *accelerated* my personal development by 20 years. **I've accomplished things that I struggled with for many, many years.** I got them accomplished in months by using this phrase. I use it in almost everything I say.

You can see it in almost all my writing. And not only does it feel good to say, but it's true. All I want to do is keep on affirming truth.

You may have said in the past, "I am a millionaire. **I am a millionaire**. I am a millionaire."

And you're not.

Because of cognitive dissonance, whatever is more true gets fired in your neural network so your thoughts instead turn to these phrases:

- "I am not a millionaire."
- "I am going to act like I am not a millionaire."
- "I am going to spend money like a person who is not a millionaire."
- "I am not going to think like a millionaire."

Your body sends a message to your mind: this phrase is not true. What gets implanted is this: "I am not a millionaire."

However, when you change your affirmation to a simple statement, "I love the thought that I am a millionaire," there is no cognitive dissonance because that statement is true.

"I love the thought that I am a millionaire."

This completely true statement bypasses the critical mind and gets implanted.

I also like to use the phrase, "**Thinking about it now,**" followed by the affirmation. **This is actually a hypnosis technique, which brings into awareness the fact that you're thinking about it now.**

What I am really teaching you is self-hypnosis. I *love* the thought that I am thinking right now: you're learning to hypnotize yourself.

But don't forget what Spider-Man said, "With great power comes great responsibility." As you learn how to hypnotize yourself, you have the great responsibility to choose the words that will create what you want.

My Most Inspiring Thoughts on Creating Wealth, Growing Your Business and Being the Best in the World at What You Do!

What I want is for you to create wealth, grow your business, be highly productive, and become the best version of yourself.

To help you achieve this outcome, I've compiled for you 462 of my best thoughts, ideas, concepts, insights, and methods that I have mastered.

You can find all these affirmations in my book "**I Love the Thought That**..."

You can get a copy at Amazon.com. I love that thought.

This is my promise to you: when you invest the time and effort into reading these affirmations regularly, you will eventually create all the wealth you desire, grow your business as large as you want, and become the best in the world at what you do!

I love that thought.

I wrote this thought out every day—over and over—until it became true.

Thinking about it now, I love the thought that I'm A CrossFit Games Athlete.

I love the thought that I qualified to go to the CrossFit Games.

I wrote these two affirmations at least 5,000 times in my journals. I would close my eyes and visualize it over and over again. You can achieve anything you conceive if you believe.

And how do you develop the belief?

Over and over and over again.

And how do you know you believe it?

You'll achieve it.

If it's not achieved, you don't have enough belief.

That's the beautiful thing about achievement. Achievement is the direct reflection of what you believe.

And if it has not been manifested, if it has not brought from the formless void through to the form of reality, what's missing is belief.

Belief makes everything that is impossible, possible. Everything.

When you have this insightful understanding, you will look at your life as a perfect reflection of what you believe.

My business is a reflection of what I believe. My financial situation is a reflection of what I believe.

That's all it is.

This is not a strategy to get skinny, rich, and happy. If you want to be skinny, rich, and happy, stop looking for how to do that.

You can go onto Amazon and type, "how to be rich, skinny, and happy." There are 27 million books on strategies for how to be skinny, rich, and happy.

What's missing is the deep belief that you are skinny, rich, and happy.

Chapter 3: Team Of Believers

Alone you can go fast; with a team, you can go far.
—Anonymous

Get A Coach

"A Coach is part adviser, part sounding board, part cheerleader, part manager and part strategist."

—The Business Journal

Because I've been coaching business people for more than 30 years—long before the concept of coaching was mainstream—I know the value that a coach can bring into your life.

The first person I looked for was my coach. I've had several CrossFit Coaches over the years, so I knew what I wanted and what I didn't want.

I interviewed three different coaches.

My interview went like this:

I believe that I can qualify for the CrossFit Games and I am looking for a coach to get me there. Are you that person?

The first guy said, "Do you have any idea how hard that is going to be?"

Next.

The Second guy said, "I've never gotten anyone to the Games in the past, let me think about it."

Next.

Then I met Coach **Dave Cowan, owner of CrossFit Sebastopol.** He said, "Let me see you train today and if I like what I see, I'll get you to the Game." Hired!

This is the reality. If you want to make the impossible possible, you MUST have a coach who believes in you as much or more than you believe in yourself.

Nobody does anything impossible on their own.

A coach won't do the work for you, but he/she will...

Be your confidant. When you challenge yourself to live outside your comfort zone, your coach will patiently and persistently hold the space for you to grow incrementally. Over time, Dave discovered my fears, and helped me face and embrace them.

See your blind spots. We all have areas that are out of our awareness. Dave noticed that whenever the training called for muscle-ups, I would slow down, hesitate, and start thinking more. He was right to encourage me to aggressively approach the rings quickly. It made all the difference. One simple shift in how I approached this movement improved my performance by 100%. A coach is perfectly poised to perform this critical function.

Give objective feedback without an agenda. Since Dave and I had the same goal—Qualify for the Games—I knew he had my best interests in mind by providing me feedback and counsel.

Keep you accountable. Each day we trained, we kept a victory journal. A victory could be measured in how fast I did a workout, how much weight I lifted, or how fluidly I moved. He held me accountable for gaining a victory a day.

Get the Best Advisors

An expert advisor is a person who has a proven game plan that you and your coach agree to follow. On Dave's recommendation, we hired Ben Bergeron, owner of CrossFit New England, to provide the roadmap to the Games.

In 2016, he started a service: selling his daily training program to athletes over 60 years old.

A key piece in the puzzle of going from conceiving to achieving is that somebody must believe that they know how to get you there. Up until now, I never had that person in my life; I was flying solo on this mission. Remember, Jim Phelps had the IMF team to accomplish the impossible missions.

Every day, Coach Bergeron gave us our daily training program. Coach Dave and I would simply follow the program exactly as designed. Ben delivered it in a way that made us believe he knew what it would take to get me to the Games, far better than Dave and I did.

He had the map and enough experience with prior athletes, so he could say, "Follow my plan, because my plan has gotten over 100 people to the CrossFit Games." We didn't have to think anymore. We had the plan. All we had to do was execute.

I love the thought that when the student is ready—meaning you believe you can do it—then (and only then) the teacher appears.

I believed I could qualify for the Games, and Dave and Ben appeared.

Get Great Training Partner(s)

About a month into our training, Coach Dave invited Charlie the Monk to join us. Coach Dave said, "Joe, you need younger, better athletes to compete against daily to push you to the next level."

Charlie, a 49-year old Zen Priest who loves CrossFit and is built like a Sherman Tank joined our team. Charlie's job was to beat me in every workout. He was more than happy to kick my ass, so he obliged.

Training with another person who is better than you is a great way to push yourself past your comfort zone.

I found that my rest time was always shorter with Charlie, and I would push the weights a little heavier. Whether we realize it or not, we tend to be more aware of our training capacity and push a bit harder if we see someone else killing it.

I asked Dave why he had a guy competing against me who is much younger, stronger, and faster. Dave's answer was brilliant: "If you're the best athlete in the gym, you have no one to chase, and if you're not chasing someone, you never know how much faster you can go."

He was right.

Get A Recovery Team

I quickly discovered that what I did in between workouts was as important as what I did during the workout. Only I could control how much and how deep I slept, and what and when I ate. But the two things that really helped, which I could not do on my own, were weekly massages and a weekly visit to my chiropractor.

Madeline Gunderson is my masseuse. She is a strong, 6'1", brilliant woman from Sweden; she is trained to work with high-end athletes like I had come to believe I am. She would come to my home every Sunday at 5:00 pm and move the lactic acid which had built up in my muscle tissue.

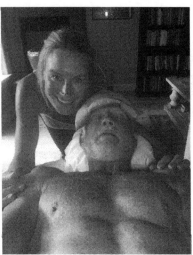

At first, I thought this was a luxury, but over time, I found it to be a necessity. After a 90-minute massage, I would sleep for 10 solid hours. During sleep, our muscles heal.

Kevin Lindsey of Performance Wellness Center in Petaluma is my chiropractor. He is a former college football player and former member of the U.S. National Rugby team. One tough dude.

He knows how to decompress athletes. Kevin says a spinal adjustment is what flossing is to teeth. The only teeth you don't floss are the ones you don't want to keep.

With Kevin and Madeline on the "Joey Team", I now understood what John Assaraf told me many years ago. "We move in the direction of the five or six people we trust the most and spend the most time with." Dave, Charlie, Kevin, and Madeline, to some degree, were my IMF that helped me make the impossible possible.

So these are a few necessary questions.

- Who is on your team?
- Is it time for you to get a coach?
- Is it time for you to get an expert advisor?
- Is it time for you to get partners to push you?
- Is it time for you to get a recovery team?

When you believe in yourself and surround yourself with others who believe in you, you stack the deck in your favor.

I have followed the same formula in business.

Over the last 30 years, I founded my company *By Referral Only* and built it to be one of the largest real estate coaching companies in the world.

When someone asks me how I did it, I always say:

"I was smart enough to know that the coach needs a coach more than anyone else. I have always looked for and hired the best business coaches available. No matter what the cost."

I am humble enough to know there are expert advisors who know a lot more about business than I do. When I need direction, I seek them out and pay for their advice.

I have been around long enough to realize that having a small team of people to work with always gets the best out of me because I want to prove to them that I can deliver.

Take a closer look at my company, **ByReferralOnly.com**, and you'll see how a small group of elite business people make the impossible possible.

Chapter 4: Private Victory Leads To Public Victory

The key factor between successful people and everyone else is that they endure, even seek out, short-term pain for long-term gain. While unsuccessful people give into, and even seek out short-term pleasure and experience long-term pain. —Ben Bergeron

I realized there were four things that I did privately which gave me short-term pleasure, but were causing me long-term pain and holding me back from long-term gain.

1. Enjoying Distractions

At the time of my CrossFit conception, I was living in downtown Encinitas, California. During the middle of the day, I got a lot of short-term pleasure by walking around the block and saying hello to everyone. I was like the mayor; everyone knew me.

I would sit and chat. I had 100 friends in the neighborhood. I could go out anytime during the day and have a meaningless dialogue, and it felt good.

But I wasn't getting the work done that needed to get done for me to train at a high level and run my multi-million-dollar business, *By Referral Only*.

One of the obstacles to achieving my impossible was my environment, which is always stronger than willpower. I had to create a new environment. That is when I decided to move to Forestville, California.

I found a beautiful home on three acres where I could build a training gym. Being around people required me to get in my car and drive 15 minutes to the closest public setting. Living in Forestville created solitude.

I needed to experience solitude.

In solitude, there is some pain. I had to embrace that pain of being unable just to walk down the street and get distracted by meeting 25 people that I knew.

But the long-term gain was to be more focused.

2. **My Sleep Pattern**

I had a habit of watching Netflix in bed at night. I would get involved in a series like *Breaking Bad* and would watch one more episode. It gave me short-term pleasure, but in the morning, I suffered the pain. I stopped doing that.

3. **Having the Second Cookie**

Because I was training so hard, I had a thought that I could enjoy sugar. This was short-term pleasure, but the inflammation and the recovery time was creating long-term pain. I stopped that.

4. **Enjoying a Cigar**

I enjoy smoking a cigar while I write. It's a ritual I developed over the past 10 years. It gives short-term pleasure, but in training to be the fittest man on Earth, it was causing me long-term pain. I stopped that.

The day I read Ben's quote, I had deep insightful understanding.

Instead of working toward getting to the Games, I would work privately on removing the habits and routines that were obstacles in my way of getting to the Games. And I did it because I believed that I was a CrossFit Games Athlete, and I was willing to do whatever it took to make my impossible possible.

I love that thought.

Celaladin Mehmet Rumi, the Persian poet, said it best: "Your task is not to seek for love, but merely to seek and find all the barriers within yourself that you have built against it."

My task was to not seek qualifying, but merely seek and find all the barriers within myself that would hold me back from qualifying.

So, I asked a question of myself before I turned on Netflix, ate sugar, or smoked a cigar: Is this giving me short-term pleasure at the price of long-term gain?

These were my private victories.

Make a list of all the things that are short-term pleasures and then ask yourself:

"Is short-term pleasure holding me back from achieving what I've conceived?"

When you look at your life and your business, where are the areas you experience that give short-term pleasure?

Our intention is to achieve something that appears impossible today, but through belief, it can become possible. The deeper truth is that you can see what you're thinking by how you're behaving. Our behavior produces the result.

Remember this:

- Thoughts create beliefs.
- Beliefs create behaviors.
- Behaviors create results.

Chapter 5: The Courageous Step Of Going Public

Once I was committed to removing the blocks to being a CrossFit Games Athlete, it was time to go public. I had started a CrossFit Journal on Facebook: "The Road to The CrossFit Games".

I posted something almost every day for three months, but I didn't push the "public" button until I had passed the thirty-day mark of no Netflix, no sugar, and no cigars. It took me three months of deep private work to let go of these addictions.

On my Freedom Day, I pressed "Public". Now I couldn't turn around. Within a month, more than 400 people were following my daily posts and watching my training videos. Some videos had a thousand views. You can check it out on the site (**www.facebook.com/CrossFitMastersJourney**).

My mission took on an entirely different meaning. Now I was inspiring hundreds of people to do *their* impossible. I was getting encouragement and acknowledgment every day. I wasn't going to let them down or myself. I believed I could do it with every fiber of my being.

It seems to me that the greatest risk in life is risking nothing. I wonder if you have something that you've conceived, but only you know about it?

What is your fear?

You cannot let fear of failure hold you back from becoming the person you choose to be. It's not possible to become the highest version of yourself without risking failure.

You must take the risk, and it's hard work. Success means taking the risk when you don't want to do it. It means taking the risk when it's uncomfortable. It means doing what is uncommon to you, what is frightening to you.

Becoming a CrossFit Games Athlete taught me to challenge myself to grow through my fear by being willing to risk failure. I learned to be willing to test my capacity.

I learned that success is who I become while I fail and keep picking myself up and doing it again.

I learned to aggressively fail.

We have only one life—risk living it fully.

We are here to grow **better.**

We are here to grow **smarter.**

We are here to grow **wiser**.

We are here to ask more of ourselves.

We are here to ask more of the universe.

We are here to find our unique voice, our unique ideas, and our unique contribution; the only way is by risking failure, by being fully vulnerable.

You don't have to be fearless. Courage is not the absence of fear. Courage is the willingness to act in the midst of fear. The person who risks nothing does nothing, has nothing, is nothing, and becomes nothing. You may avoid suffering and sorrow. But you simply cannot learn, feel, change, grow, love, and live.

Again, the greatest risk in life is risking nothing.

It's a huge risk to go public because of the fear involved for all of us—the fear of embarrassment, the fear of failure, and the fear of public ridicule.

So look into your experience and ask yourself:

- What do you want to achieve?
- What can you do now to strengthen your belief?
- What private work needs to occur before it becomes public?
- Once you've made that commitment, will you risk going public?

I trained hard for 10 months, five days a week, for two to four hours a day. Throughout the year, I had many significant, insightful understandings about what it takes to make the impossible possible, but these are my top 10.

Chapter 6: Top 10 Insights On The Road To Qualifying For The CrossFit Games

1. **Having a reason is more important than knowing how**. Every day, I asked myself one simple question: "Joe, what is important about qualifying for the 2017 CrossFit Games, to you?" Each day, my "why" became stronger and stronger, until one day, I answered the question: because I said I would. Keeping my word to myself became my motivation and personal inspiration.

2. **The will to prepare to win is more important than the will to win.** When I focused on winning, I was comparing myself to others. When I focused on preparing to win, I worked on my weakness and got better. In the CrossFit world, it is better to be really good at everything than it is to be amazing at a few things and suck at others.

3. **It's called the CrossFit *Games*.** I kept reminding myself that this was not my life, but a game I was playing. Once the game is over, all the kings and pawns all go back in the same box. This mindset made it more fun and gave me the ability to laugh at myself when I would take things too seriously.

4. **We don't get rid of our demons, we just get above them when we need to.** I love that line from the movie *Dr. Strange*. My demons of distraction—Netflix, sugar, and cigars—are still there, but I've learned to use them as inspiration to become a better man and not beat myself up for being human.

5. **The way I do anything is the way I do everything.** Everything counts. How I make my bed is the same way I do everything. When I pay attention to details in the trivial part of my life, I pay even more attention when it matters most.

6. **I don't have to love the training, but I do need to believe it's worth it.** There were long hours of recovery and hurting in every bone of my body, but I truly believed it was worth it.

7. **Everything in my life becomes easier when I stop expecting it to be easy.** Qualifying for the Games was the hardest thing I've ever done. I've done some tough stuff. I've stayed in business for more than 35 years through every type of economy. I've been married twice. I was the oldest guy to make it through Kokoro, which is the civilian version of the Navy Seal Hell Week. I've climbed to 18,000 feet with a group of people who were

very unprepared for that journey. I know difficulty, and I've come to believe all the things I want in life are outside my comfort zone.

8. **When I ask myself, "What do I do next?" it is usually the step that I don't want to take.** So, I started asking, "What do I *not* want to do?" Then I would do that. It helps develop resilience and courage.

9. **"Instant results" is an illusion.** If anyone wants to sell you on instant abs, or instant millions, run away from it as fast you can. It takes work. But most importantly, it's not about the abs or becoming a millionaire—I have achieved both goals—the most important part is who you become along the way.

10. **A belief is nothing more than a thought you repeat over and over again.** What you think about and what you talk about, you bring about.

Chapter 7: The Rest Of The Story

Two weeks before the CrossFit Games in Madison, I was training by doing heavy dumbbell snatch work, when I heard a pop in my shoulder.

I couldn't move my shoulder over my head without searing pain. I went and got X-rays.

My shoulder was bone-on-bone and the nerve in between the bone was being pinched.

I asked for cortisone to get me through.

The doctor refused and said, "This shoulder needs two to three months of rest or you will not be able to put your own luggage in the overhead on an airplane, and you will never be able to pick up your grandchildren."

He showed me the Level 1 tear in my rotator cuff. If it ripped, recovery would take a year after surgery.

What he didn't know was that the CrossFit Games started in 11 days.

So I told him. He said, "You would be crazy to do that to yourself."

It was a surreal experience.

At first, I thought, "Okay, I'll find another doctor who will give me the cortisone shots." I went home. I did what I always do when my mind is racing and I'm projecting negative energy. I sat in my meditation chair. I got still.

I wrote this question in my journal: "What's important about risking damaging your shoulder by going to the CrossFit Games?" My first thought was, "Because I've trained so hard to get here, it would all be wasted."

Then I asked, "Is that true?"

The answer was, "Not at all." It was not wasted. At the age of 60, I was one of the 20 fittest men on Earth. I had made remarkable lifelong friends. I had inspired hundreds of people.

Then I would ask again: "What's important about risking damaging your shoulder by going to the CrossFit Games?"

I would answer it, then ask, "Is that true?"

After an hour of this, I called my life-long advisor, Larry Laveman, and shared with him what I was processing.

He said, "Joe, you have mastered the art of 'Not Quitting'. What you have to learn from this is the difference between quitting and being complete. Your body is complete, your mind will never be. It's time to listen to your body, not your mind."

It was a tough choice, but I choose to not compete.

However, I realized I had achieved what I set out to do. I had qualified for the CrossFit Games and I was at peace with that choice.

It's time for a new mission.

Chapter 8: Imagine Your Impossible

What is something that you've been wanting to do or become, but because of a limiting belief, you've considered it impossible?

For a few examples:

- Run a marathon.
- Hike the Spanish Trail.
- Travel around the world.
- Find your perfect partner.
- Live anywhere in the world for one year.
- Write a book.
- Do good Kokoro.
- Qualify for the CrossFit Games.
- Start your own company.

When you look into your own experience, no doubt, there is something within you that you would love to birth.

Once you've conceived it, then use the coaching session and the Self-Facilitation Worksheet I've created for you. It will help you to strengthen your belief, identify your obstacles, and create a plan to go public. With your willingness and your courage, nothing—absolutely nothing—is impossible.

Thank you for your time and attention, your thoughts, and your comments are welcome. You can email me at **NHVjoe@gmail.com.**

Impossible Made Possible Coaching Session

Joe: What can you imagine—something that seems impossible now that you want to make possible?

Client: I've wanted to run a marathon for the last 5 years, but don't believe I can make it.

Joe: Is running a marathon important to you?

Client: Yes.

Joe: To you, what is important about running a marathon?

Client: My husband and son do it and I would like to be part of that experience with them.

Joe: To you, what is important about being part of that experience?

Client: It's time I get involved with them. They invite me in, but I always say I can't.

Joe: What is important about being involved with them as a family?

Client: They seem so much closer to each other, and I feel like I'm outside looking in. I want to be in.

Joe: To you, what is important about being 'in'?

Client: I love them both so much and this is my way of showing love.

Joe: Do you believe that training and running the marathon will bring you closer together as a family, and help you express your love?

Client: I do.

Joe: What are the roadblocks or habits stopping you from expressing your love and doing the work to run a marathon?

Client: I don't want to fail.

Joe: What would failure look like?

Client: Not finishing the race.

Joe: What blocks do you believe are in the way of you finishing?

Client: I don't like to run, but the truth is that I have never really done much running.

Joe: What is the block?

Client: I have to stop telling myself I don't like to run because I don't even know if that is true.

Joe: What is a more honest story you could tell yourself?

Client: That I will find out if I like to run by running.

Joe: What other habits do you have to develop? Look at the habits your husband and son have developed.

Client: They have a plan and they stick to it, no matter what.

Joe: What happens when you imagine yourself having a plan and sticking to it?

Client: I actually get excited.

Joe: Do you think that most marathon runners have a plan?

Client: Yes.

Joe: So, if you had a plan, you would be a marathon runner?

Client: That's right.

Joe: Would you be willing to ask your husband and son to share their plan with you, and do you think they would?

Client: They would love to.

Joe: What other habits and rituals do you need to stop doing to believe you're a marathon runner?

Client: They run in the morning and I like to sleep in.

Joe: Would you be willing to express your love for them by giving up the short-term pleasure of sleeping in for a few months, get up earlier, and run with them for the long-term gain of being closer as a family?

Client: Well if you put it that way, of course.

Joe: That's a step in the right direction. What would be the next step? The one you don't want to take, the one that requires the most courage right now?

Client: That's easy: tell them I would love to train with them to run the marathon.

Joe: When is the best time to tell them?

Client: That's funny. I guess right now.

Joe: Let's call them now and let them know. Let's go public, shall we?

Self-Facilitation Worksheet

What can you imagine now that seems impossible now that you want to make possible?

1. _____

What's important about **1.** _____ to you?

2. _____

What's important about **2.** _____ to you?

3. _____

What's important about **3.** _____ to you?

4. _____

What's important about **4.** _____ to you?

5. _____

What's important about **5.** _____ to you?

6. _____

What's important about **6.** _____ to you?

7. _____

What's important about **7.** _____ to you?

Do you believe that **1.** _____ will give you

5. _____ **6.** _____ **7.** _____

What are the roadblock or habits that are stopping you?

a. _____

What would **a.** _____ look like?

What is a more honest story you could tell yourself about **a.**?

_____

What happens when you imagine yourself?

1. _____

Getting From Where You Are To Where You Want To Be Is Your Mission.

"Everything in my life became easier when I stop expecting it to be easy." - Joe Stumpf

Successful people take on seemingly impossible missions because they believe they are here to impact others and make their mark in the world.

Anything and everything is possible. The more difficult and challenging the mission, the stronger and wiser your team must be.

These are three ways you can put me on your team today:

1. Subscribe to my **DailyInspiredActions.com** morning email. Every morning you will find in your inbox a specific action step you can take to make your impossible possible. It's free.

2. Get a Free Copy of my book **Inside Secrets;** What the World's Best Real Estate Agents Are Doing Today to Get Even Better. Email me at **NHVjoe@gmail.com.**

Three More Great Books By Joe Stumpf

Willing Warrior - Surviving the Civilian Version of the Navy SEAL Hell Week at the Age of 54!

My story about the 21 life lessons learned while becoming one of the oldest guys to ever survive the civilian version of the Navy SEAL Hell Week. As a special bonus when you order this book, send me a quick email to **NHVjoe@gmail.com** and I'll send you a link to a 30-minute live Willing Warrior video presentation that teaches you how to apply these lessons in your life and business. Thank you - Hoooyaaaa!

I Love the Thought That...: My Most Inspiring Thoughts on Creating Wealth, Growing Your Business, and Being the Best in the World at What You Do!

An affirmation is a suggestion you make to yourself that is carefully crafted as a statement of a desirable intention you want to deliberately create. By consciously meditating and dwelling on it, through constantly repeating the statement and visualizing it as true, you automatically implant the affirmation so it becomes part of who you want to be. When practiced deliberately and repeatedly, affirmations regularly reinforce the chemical pathway of your brain to make the neurons connecting to your statement stronger.

In this book, I give you 463 of my most inspiring affirmations on creating wealth, growing your business and being the best in the world at what you do.

The Path to Authentic Power: How to Make the Changes That Change Everything

Change is about stripping the mask away. My hope is that by the time you are done reading this, you will have a deeper understanding of how enormous the personal implications are when you say, "I want to change." When you say, "I want to change," what you're really talking about are your habits. The habits that are conditioned in your childhood. Even more ingrained are the habits that come from the deep, evolutionary, primitive past. We grow personally when we step up and we take intelligent, healthy risks. Actually, you know in your own experience that the real juice in life is when you take off the "play it safe" mask and you allow yourself to be energized by the challenge.

You can find all Joe's book at Amazon.com

66329854R00040

Made in the USA
San Bernardino, CA
11 January 2018